WELCOME TO THE U.S.A.
KANSAS

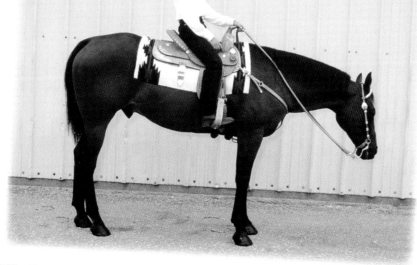

Written by Ann Heinrichs   Illustrated by Matt Kania
Content Adviser: Lois Herr, Education Coordinator,
Kansas State Historical Society, Topeka, Kansas

The Child's World

Published in the United States of America by The Child's World®
PO Box 326 • Chanhassen, MN 55317-0326
800-599-READ • www.childsworld.com

Photo Credits
Cover: Medioimages; frontispiece: Philip Gould/Corbis.

Interior: Bettmann/Corbis: 14, 18; Corbis: 6 (David Muench), 9 (David A. Northcott), 10 (W. Perry Conway), 13 (Jonathan Blair); Fiesta Mexicana: 25; Getty Images/Hulton|Archive/Pictorial Parade: 20; Philip Gould/Corbis: 22, 33; Dave G. Houser/Corbis: 17, 21; Library of Congress: 28; Gavin Peters/Exploration Place: 29; Picture Desk: 19 (The Art Archive/Culver Pictures), 26 (Travelsite/Global); Professor Sonny Ramaswamy/Kansas State University: 34; Russell Stover Candies: 30.

Acknowledgments
The Child's World®: Mary Berendes, Publishing Director

Editorial Directions, Inc.: E. Russell Primm, Editorial Director; Katie Marsico, Associate Editor; Judith Shiffer, Assistant Editor; Matt Messbarger, Editorial Assistant; Susan Hindman, Copy Editor; Melissa McDaniel, Proofreader; Kevin Cunningham, Peter Garnham, Matt Messbarger, Olivia Nellums, Chris Simms, Molly Symmonds, Katherine Trickle, Carl Stephen Wender, Fact Checkers; Tim Griffin/IndexServ, Indexer; Cian Loughlin O'Day, Photo Researcher and Editor

The Design Lab: Kathleen Petelinsek, Design and art production

Library of Congress Cataloging-in-Publication Data
Heinrichs, Ann.
Kansas / by Ann Heinrichs.
    p. cm. — (Welcome to the U.S.A.)
Includes index.
ISBN 1-59296-443-5 (library bound : alk. paper) 1. Kansas—Juvenile literature. I. Title.
F681.3.H453 2006
978.1—dc22   2005000519

Ann Heinrichs is the author of more than 100 books for children and young adults. She has also enjoyed successful careers as a children's book editor and an advertising copywriter. Ann grew up in Fort Smith, Arkansas, and lives in Chicago, Illinois.

About the Author
Ann Heinrichs

Matt Kania loves maps and, as a kid, dreamed of making them. In school he studied geography and cartography, and today he makes maps for a living. Matt's favorite thing about drawing maps is learning about the places they represent. Many of the maps he has created can be found in books, magazines, videos, Web sites, and public places.

About the
Map Illustrator
Matt Kania

On the cover: **Scarecrows protect a field of sunflowers.**
On page one: **This horse and rider are ready to compete at the Kansas State Fair.**

OUR KANSAS TRIP

Kansas's Nicknames: The Sunflower State and the Jayhawk State

4

et's take a trip through Kansas! You'll find lots to see and do there.

You'll meet Wyatt Earp, gunfighters, and outlaws. You'll ride stagecoaches and trains. You'll pet a bug and fly a plane. You'll spot dinosaurs and prairie dogs. And you'll even see a fish inside a fish.

Does this sound like your kind of fun? Then hop in and buckle up tight. Let's hit the road!

WELCOME TO KANSAS

As you travel through Kansas, watch for all the interesting facts along the way.

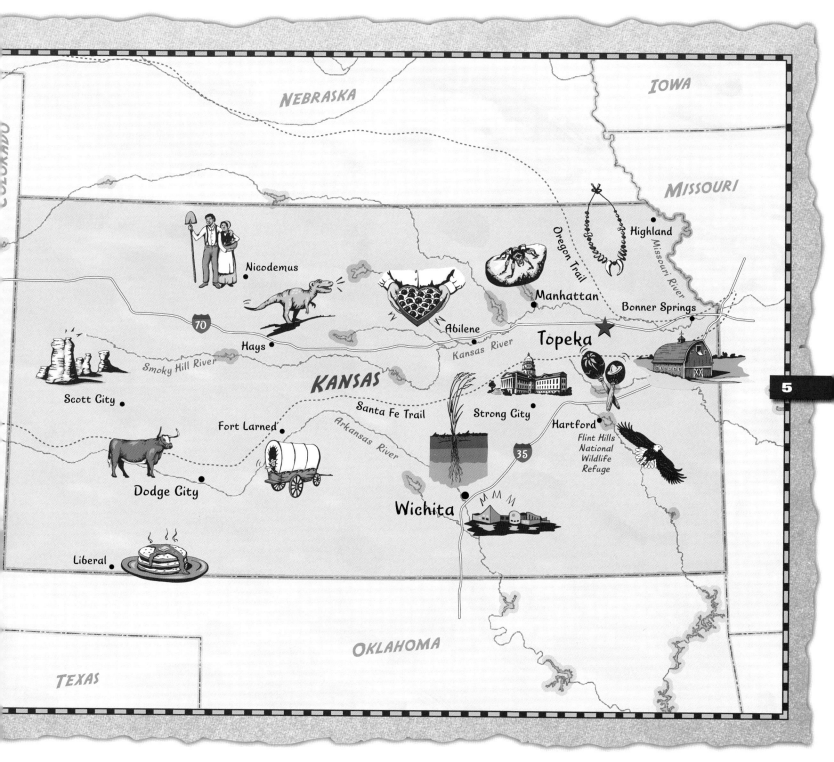

NEBRASKA

IOWA

COLORADO

MISSOURI

Nicodemus

Highland

Missouri River

Oregon Trail

Manhattan

Bonner Springs

70

Abilene

Topeka

Hays

Kansas River

Smoky Hill River

KANSAS

5

Scott City

Santa Fe Trail

Strong City

Hartford

Fort Larned

Arkansas River

35

Flint Hills
National
Wildlife
Refuge

Dodge City

Wichita

Liberal

OKLAHOMA

TEXAS

Don't forget to visit Monument Rocks. It's almost like walking through a giant maze!

6

Milford Lake is Kansas's largest lake. It was created on the Republican River.

The rocks tower high overhead. Some are as tall as seven-story buildings. Some have big holes. You can walk through these holes. It's almost as if they were doors!

You're wandering around Monument Rocks near Scott City. They rise in an area called the Badlands. A sea once covered this part of Kansas. Now, high cliffs and strange rocks stand there.

Plains cover most of Kansas. Some are gently rolling plains. Others are just plain flat!

The Arkansas and Kansas rivers run through Kansas. Many smaller rivers flow into them. Kansas has lots of lakes, too. Most were made by building dams on rivers. Water backs up behind a dam. That creates a lake.

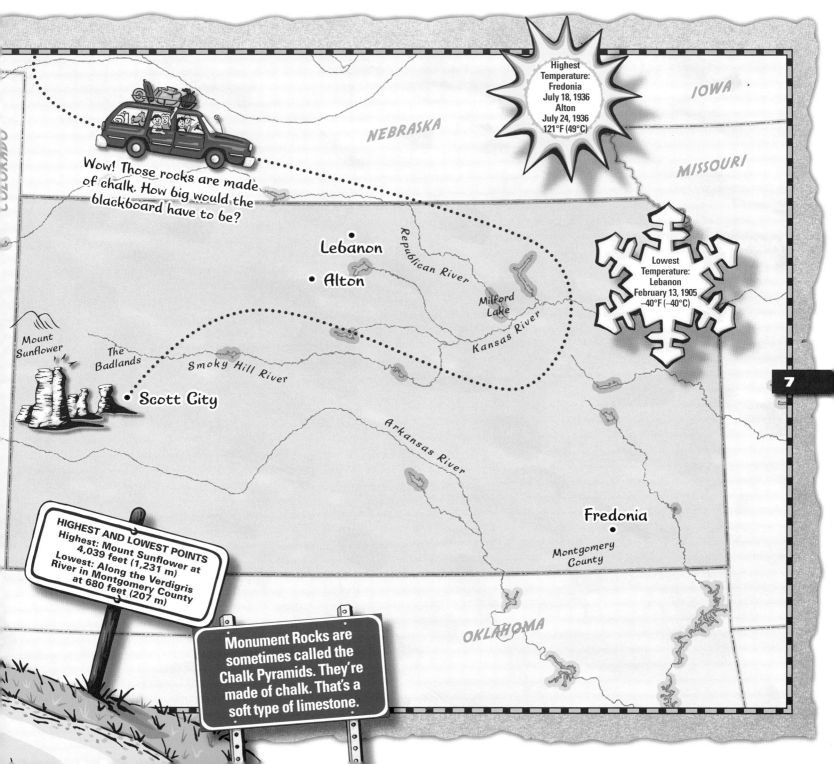

NEBRASKA

IOWA

MISSOURI

COLORADO

Highest Temperature:
Fredonia
July 18, 1936
Alton
July 24, 1936
121°F (49°C)

Lowest Temperature:
Lebanon
February 13, 1905
−40°F (−40°C)

Wow! Those rocks are made of chalk. How big would the blackboard have to be?

Lebanon

Alton

Republican River

Milford Lake

Kansas River

Mount Sunflower

The Badlands

Smoky Hill River

Scott City

Arkansas River

Fredonia

Montgomery County

HIGHEST AND LOWEST POINTS
Highest: Mount Sunflower at
4,039 feet (1,231 m)
Lowest: Along the Verdigris
River in Montgomery
County at 680 feet (207 m)

Monument Rocks are sometimes called the Chalk Pyramids. They're made of chalk. That's a soft type of limestone.

OKLAHOMA

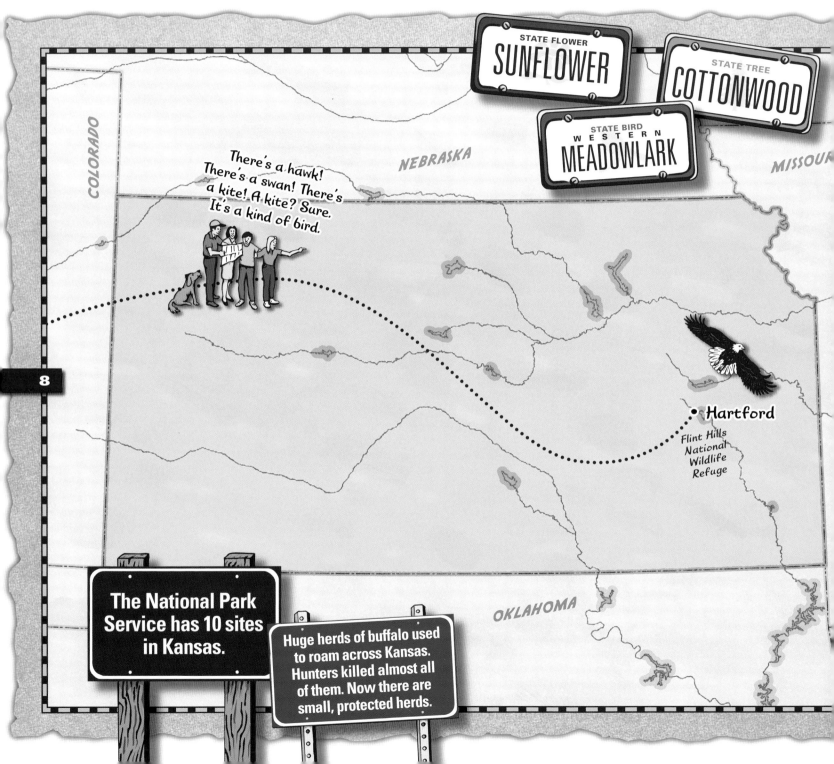

STATE FLOWER
SUNFLOWER

STATE TREE
COTTONWOOD

STATE BIRD
WESTERN
MEADOWLARK

COLORADO

NEBRASKA

MISSOURI

There's a hawk!
There's a swan! There's
a kite! A kite? Sure.
It's a kind of bird.

• Hartford

Flint Hills
National
Wildlife
Refuge

OKLAHOMA

**The National Park
Service has 10 sites
in Kansas.**

Huge herds of buffalo used
to roam across Kansas.
Hunters killed almost all
of them. Now there are
small, protected herds.

Flint Hills National Wildlife Refuge

Look out! Kansas is home to many animals, including snakes.

A deer peeks around a tree. Wild turkeys waddle through the grass. Doves are cooing, and ducks are quacking. An eagle soars overhead. You're enjoying a day with nature!

This is Flint Hills National Wildlife Refuge. It's near Hartford in southeastern Kansas. It protects thousands of wild animals.

Kansas's grasslands are home to many animals. You'll find rabbits, raccoons, and coyotes there. And you'll see foxes, weasels, and skunks.

Prairie dogs dig tunnels for homes. Groups of them live together in towns. They have to watch out for snakes. And so do you!

A coyote pup prances through Tallgrass Prairie National Preserve.

The Flint Hills have the largest area of original grasslands in Kansas.

Tall grasses once waved across the nation's plains. These grasslands are called tallgrass prairies. They were like a sea of grass. They covered much of the central United States.

Farmers plowed up most of that grass. Only a tiny bit of tallgrass prairie remains. Much of it is in Tallgrass Prairie National Preserve. It's in the Flint Hills near Strong City.

The preserve's tall grasses are taller than you. But there are short grasses, too. Many colorful prairie flowers also bloom there.

Coyotes, foxes, and deer live in the preserve. Little mice scurry among the grasses. One is the meadow jumping mouse. It's very tiny. And it jumps!

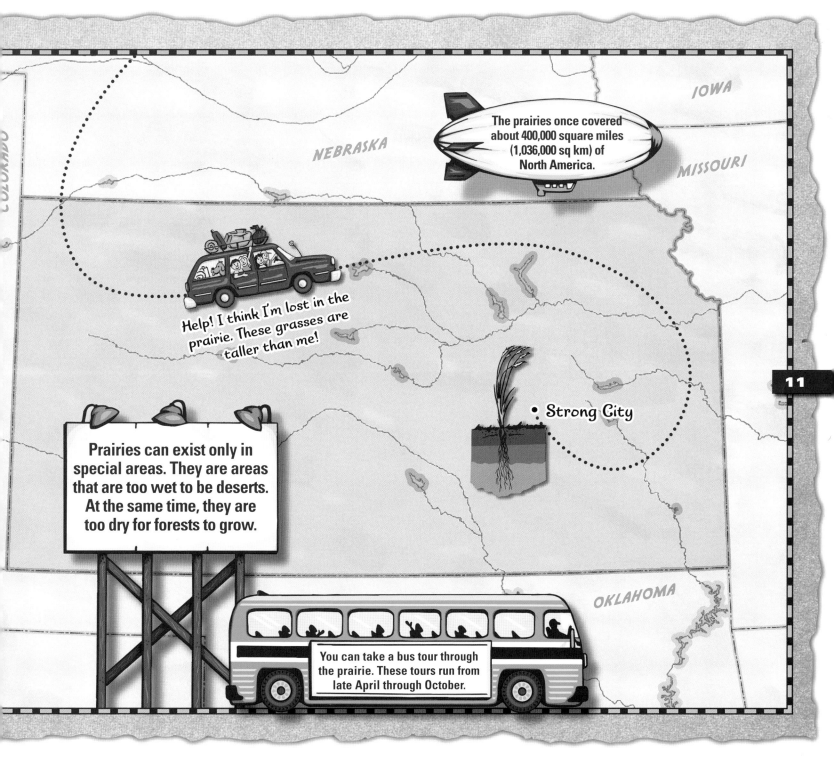

The prairies once covered about 400,000 square miles (1,036,000 sq km) of North America.

Help! I think I'm lost in the prairie. These grasses are taller than me!

Prairies can exist only in special areas. They are areas that are too wet to be deserts. At the same time, they are too dry for forests to grow.

Strong City

You can take a bus tour through the prairie. These tours run from late April through October.

IOWA

NEBRASKA

MISSOURI

COLORADO

OKLAHOMA

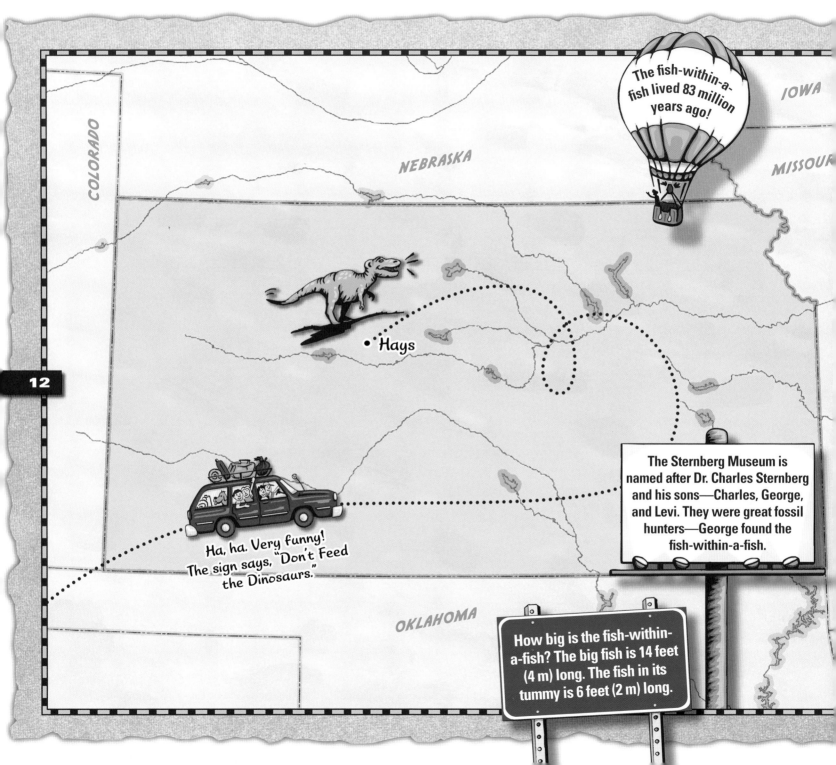

The Sternberg Museum in Hays

You'll love the Sternberg Museum of Natural History. The fun begins when you walk in. You're face-to-face with a mammoth skeleton! Mammoths were like giant elephants. They roamed the Earth thousands of years ago.

Don't forget to visit the walk-through exhibits. They're full of life-size model dinosaurs. You'll be glad they're not alive. Their sharp teeth look ready to bite!

You've got to see the famous fish-within-a-fish. It's the **fossil** skeleton of a huge fish. Inside it is a smaller fish. The big fish ate the little fish. Then the big fish died!

Yikes! It's a *Tyrannosaurus rex*! Don't worry— it's just a model at the Sternberg Museum.

Visit the museum's Discovery Room. You can touch animal fur, hold bones, and do other fun things.

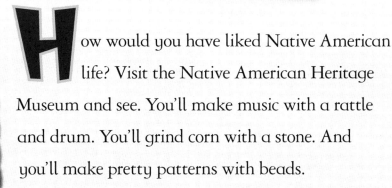

Native American Heritage Museum in Highland

The Arapahos once called Kansas home. This photo was taken in 1870 in Fort Dodge.

How would you have liked Native American life? Visit the Native American Heritage Museum and see. You'll make music with a rattle and drum. You'll grind corn with a stone. And you'll make pretty patterns with beads.

This museum explores Kansas's Indian **cultures.** Thousands of American Indians once lived in Kansas. They hunted buffalo across the plains. At home, they grew corn, beans, and squash.

French explorers claimed this region in 1682. In 1803, France sold it to the United States. The U.S. government set up **reservations** in Kansas. Indians from eastern states were moved to these reservations.

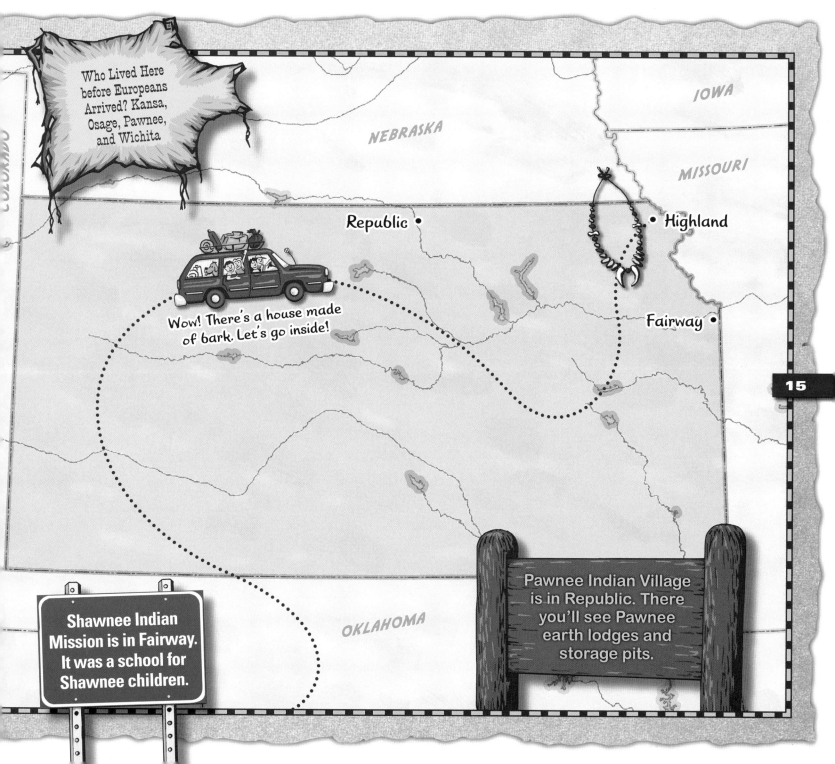

Who Lived Here before Europeans Arrived? Kansa, Osage, Pawnee, and Wichita

COLORADO

NEBRASKA

IOWA

MISSOURI

Republic

Highland

Wow! There's a house made of bark. Let's go inside!

Fairway

OKLAHOMA

15

Shawnee Indian Mission is in Fairway. It was a school for Shawnee children.

Pawnee Indian Village is in Republic. There you'll see Pawnee earth lodges and storage pits.

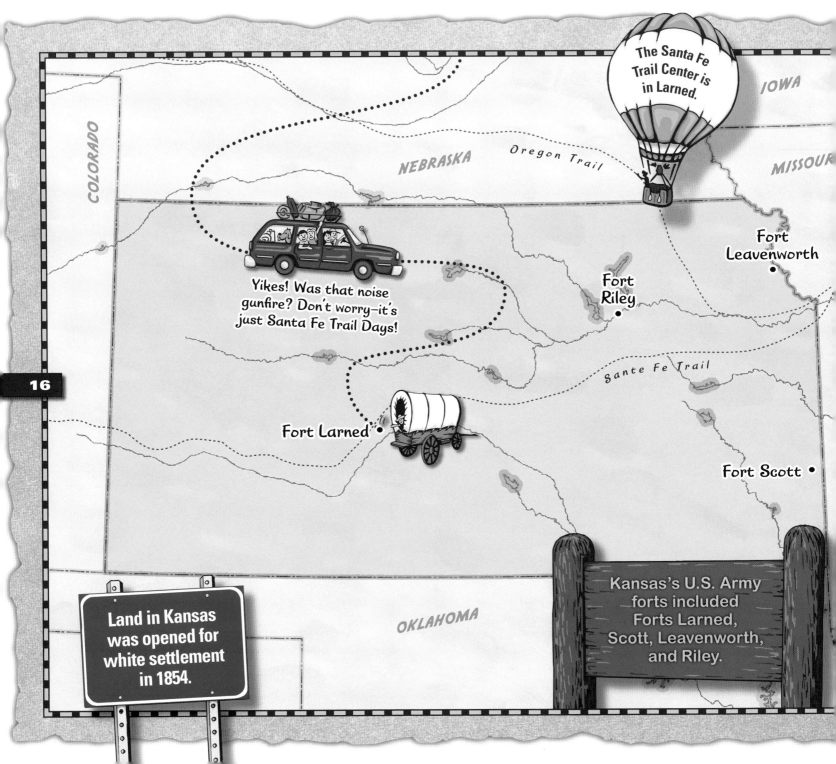

Santa Fe Trail Days at Fort Larned

This house is one of many historic attractions in Fort Larned.

The soldiers look like they're from the 1850s. They line up and march with their guns. Then, pow! They fire into the air. It's Santa Fe Trail Days at Fort Larned!

Fort Larned was one of many army forts in Kansas. Some forts protected traders and their goods in Kansas. Traders used Fort Larned when traveling on the Santa Fe Trail.

Others forts were used to protect **pioneers.** The pioneers were heading west. Some used the Oregon Trail. That trail went through northeast Kansas. The pioneers hoped to settle in a new place.

Pioneer families and traders traveled in covered wagons. The wagon wheels left deep ruts, or ditches. You can still see those ruts today!

The Santa Fe Trail opened in 1821. It ran from Independence, Missouri, to Santa Fe, New Mexico.

Kansas earned a bloody reputation during the 1850s. People fought violently about the issue of slavery.

18

Nicodemus is a special town. African Americans founded it in 1877. Before that, Northern and Southern states argued about slavery. Both sides wanted more states to agree with their view. Things got violent in the 1850s. Kansas was just about to become a state.

People from both sides came into Kansas. They tried to force their views on everyone. Some people were killed as they fought. Kansas got the nickname Bleeding Kansas.

Finally, the Civil War (1861–1865) broke out. The North won, and slavery ended. Many former slaves had nowhere to go. That's why a black minister founded Nicodemus. He invited former slaves to join him there.

You can visit Nicodemus's historic churches, town hall, school, and hotel.

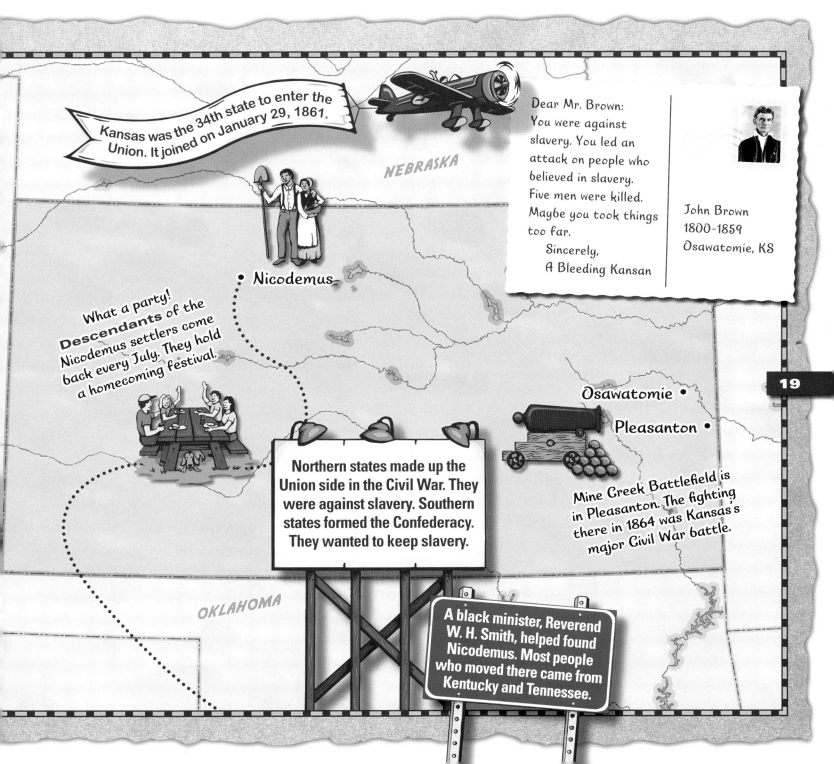

Kansas was the 34th state to enter the Union. It joined on January 29, 1861.

NEBRASKA

Dear Mr. Brown:
You were against slavery. You led an attack on people who believed in slavery. Five men were killed. Maybe you took things too far.
    Sincerely,
    A Bleeding Kansan

John Brown
1800-1859
Osawatomie, KS

• Nicodemus

What a party! **Descendants** of the Nicodemus settlers come back every July. They hold a homecoming festival.

Osawatomie •

Pleasanton •

Northern states made up the Union side in the Civil War. They were against slavery. Southern states formed the Confederacy. They wanted to keep slavery.

Mine Creek Battlefield is in Pleasanton. The fighting there in 1864 was Kansas's major Civil War battle.

OKLAHOMA

A black minister, Reverend W. H. Smith, helped found Nicodemus. Most people who moved there came from Kentucky and Tennessee.

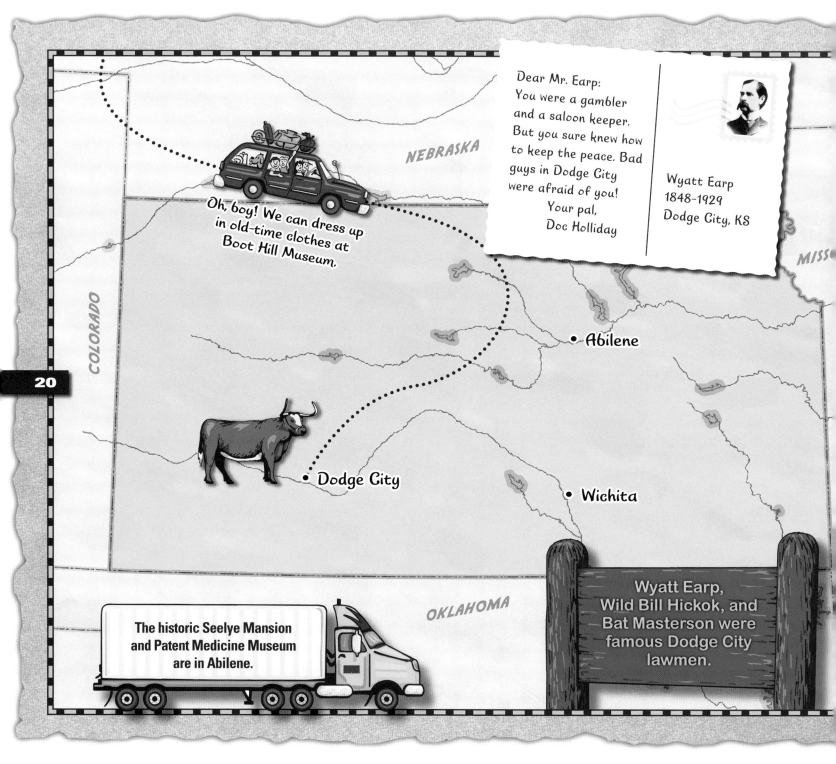

NEBRASKA

COLORADO

MISSOURI

Oh, boy! We can dress up in old-time clothes at Boot Hill Museum.

Dear Mr. Earp:
You were a gambler and a saloon keeper. But you sure knew how to keep the peace. Bad guys in Dodge City were afraid of you!
Your pal,
Doc Holliday

Wyatt Earp
1848-1929
Dodge City, KS

• Abilene

• Dodge City

• Wichita

OKLAHOMA

The historic Seelye Mansion and Patent Medicine Museum are in Abilene.

Wyatt Earp, Wild Bill Hickok, and Bat Masterson were famous Dodge City lawmen.

Dodge City and Boot Hill

Watch the gunfighters shoot it out. Ride a stagecoach around town. It's time for Dodge City Days! This festival celebrates Dodge City's cowboy past.

Cowboys drove their cattle to Kansas in the 1870s. The cattle were shipped out on railroad cars. Dodge City, Abilene, and Wichita were railroad centers. They were called cow towns.

Cowboys got pretty wild in the cow towns. Lawmen tried to keep the peace. Of course, some outlaws got shot. Many ended up in Boot Hill Cemetery in Dodge City.

Stop by the Boot Hill Museum. You'll learn all about the cowboy days. You'll see the saloon and other old buildings. And you might even see a gunfight!

Open wide! These people are acting out an old-time medicine show at Boot Hill.

21

The Old Cowtown Museum is in Wichita. It preserves buildings from Wichita's cow town days.

Wellington holds the Kansas Wheat Festival every July.

The Ag Center in Bonner Springs

Toot, toot! All aboard! You're riding a train around Farm Town USA. This town is part of a huge farm museum—the National Agricultural Center and Hall of Fame. People call it the Ag Center for short.

Farming has always been important in Kansas. Millions of beef cattle graze on the plains. Golden fields of wheat stretch across the plains, too. Mills grind that wheat into flour. Kansas grows more wheat than any other state.

A farmer in Abilene inspects his wheat crop.

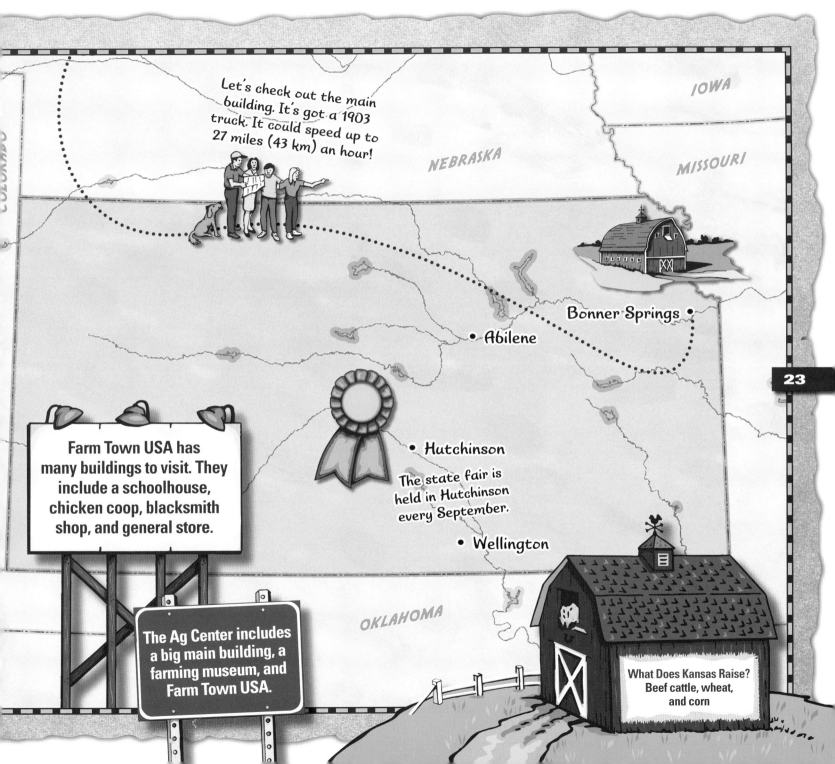

Let's check out the main building. It's got a 1903 truck. It could speed up to 27 miles (43 km) an hour!

IOWA

NEBRASKA

MISSOURI

Bonner Springs •

• Abilene

Farm Town USA has many buildings to visit. They include a schoolhouse, chicken coop, blacksmith shop, and general store.

• Hutchinson

The state fair is held in Hutchinson every September.

• Wellington

The Ag Center includes a big main building, a farming museum, and Farm Town USA.

OKLAHOMA

What Does Kansas Raise? Beef cattle, wheat, and corn

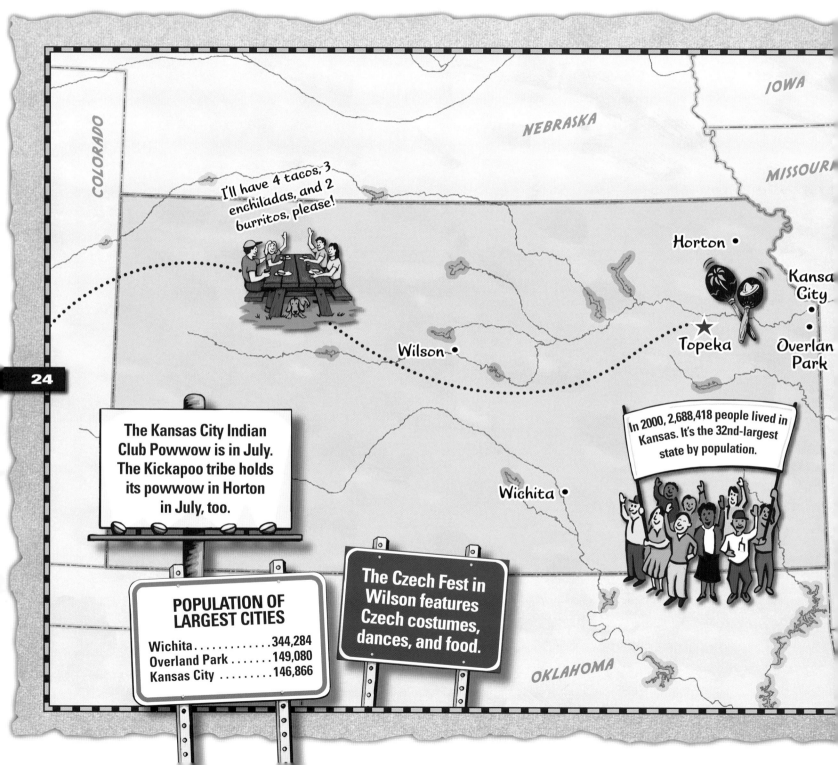

The Kansas City Indian Club Powwow is in July. The Kickapoo tribe holds its powwow in Horton in July, too.

POPULATION OF LARGEST CITIES

Wichita	344,284
Overland Park	149,080
Kansas City	146,866

The Czech Fest in Wilson features Czech costumes, dances, and food.

Topeka's Fiesta Mexicana

Do you like really hot food? Then stop by Topeka's Fiesta Mexicana. It's a five-day **Hispanic** festival. You'll eat tacos and other Mexican foods. You can even dance to a mariachi band. And here's the hot part. You can enter the **jalapeño**-eating contest. Those peppers will set your mouth on fire!

Hispanic people are one of Kansas's several **ethnic** groups. People from Germany and Sweden were early settlers. Many groups arrived in the early 1900s. They included Italians, Mexicans, and Croatians. Each group brought its native foods and customs.

Can you carry a tune? This mariachi singer performs at Fiesta Mexicana.

The State Capitol in Topeka

The capitol is full of history lessons. But you don't need to read them. Just look at them! The capitol has huge murals, or wall paintings. They show famous events in Kansas's history.

Kansas's state government offices are in the capitol. There are three branches of state government. One branch makes the laws. Another branch carries out the laws. The governor heads this branch. Judges make up the third branch. The judges meet in courts. They decide whether laws have been broken.

Kansas sure has a colorful capitol in springtime!

The Gallery of Also-Rans is in Norton. It features people who ran for president but lost.

A stone fence surrounded the state capitol in its early days. It was built to keep cows away!

Welcome to Topeka, the capital of Kansas!

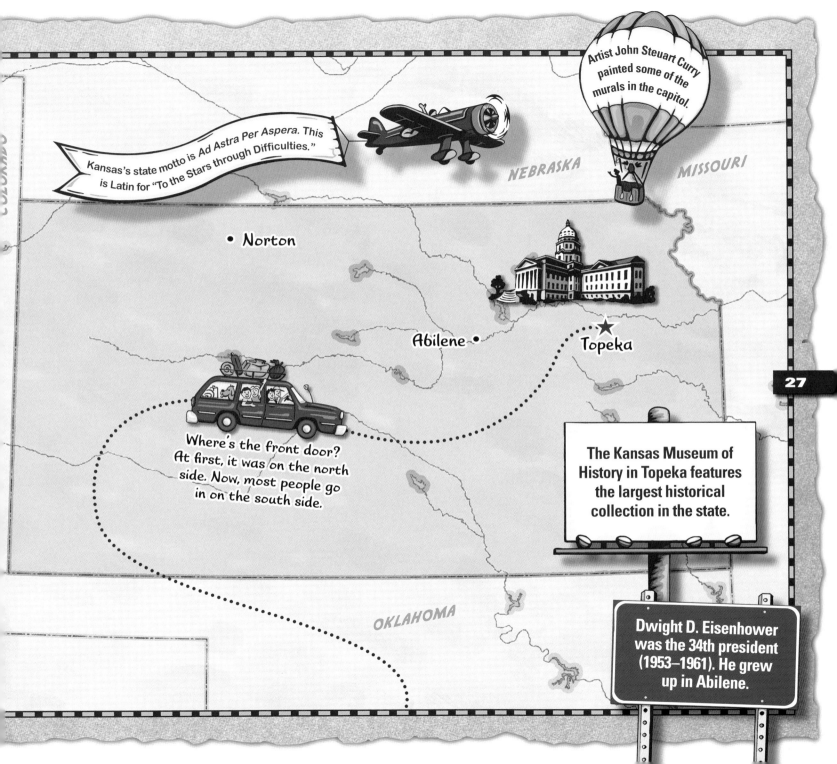

Kansas's state motto is *Ad Astra Per Aspera*. This is Latin for "To the Stars through Difficulties."

Artist John Steuart Curry painted some of the murals in the capitol.

NEBRASKA

MISSOURI

COLORADO

• Norton

Abilene •

★ Topeka

Where's the front door? At first, it was on the north side. Now, most people go in on the south side.

The Kansas Museum of History in Topeka features the largest historical collection in the state.

OKLAHOMA

Dwight D. Eisenhower was the 34th president (1953–1961). He grew up in Abilene.

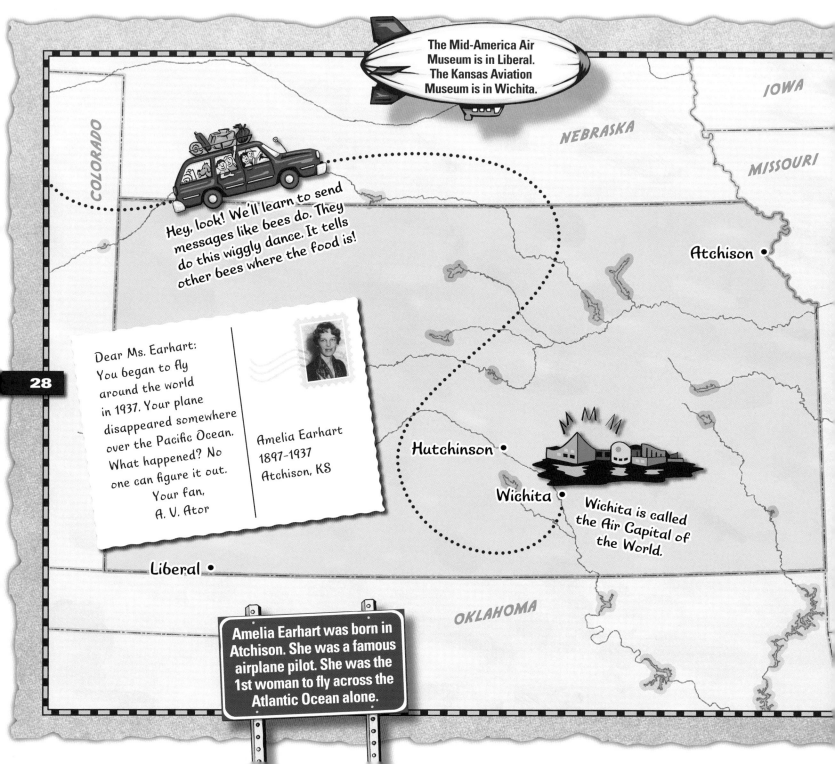

The Mid-America Air Museum is in Liberal. The Kansas Aviation Museum is in Wichita.

IOWA

COLORADO

NEBRASKA

MISSOURI

Hey, look! We'll learn to send messages like bees do. They do this wiggly dance. It tells other bees where the food is!

Atchison

Dear Ms. Earhart:
You began to fly around the world in 1937. Your plane disappeared somewhere over the Pacific Ocean. What happened? No one can figure it out.
Your fan,
A. V. Ator

Amelia Earhart
1897-1937
Atchison, KS

Hutchinson

Wichita

Wichita is called the Air Capital of the World.

Liberal

OKLAHOMA

Amelia Earhart was born in Atchison. She was a famous airplane pilot. She was the 1st woman to fly across the Atlantic Ocean alone.

Make your own airplane. Then test it in a wind tunnel. Watch a bee fly in slow motion. Now hop into an airplane pilot's seat. You'll see what it's like to fly over Kansas!

You're at Wichita's Exploration Place. It's a great science center. One section explores airplanes and flying. Just walk in and take the controls!

Airplanes are a big deal in Kansas. During World War II (1939–1945), Kansas factories built many airplanes. The U.S. government used the airplanes in the war.

Airplanes became a big industry in the state. Today, Wichita is Kansas's major aircraft center.

Do you like airplanes? Visitors examine an exhibit on air streams at Exploration Place.

29

The Kansas Cosmosphere and Space Center is in Hutchinson.

What a tasty job! Workers process candies at the Russell Stover factory in Abilene.

Russell Stover Candies in Abilene

Can you smell the chocolate? Then you're getting close to Russell Stover Candies. Come inside and take a tour. You'll see the candy cooks at work. And you'll get to eat some samples, too!

Candy is one of Kansas's many food products. Some factories make flour or animal food. Other food plants prepare beef for sale.

Airplanes are the state's leading factory goods. There are many airplane factories around Wichita. Some make military airplanes for the U.S. government. Others make small planes for private use. Kansas also makes parts for airplanes, trains, and cars.

About 1 out of 6 Kansas workers has a manufacturing job.

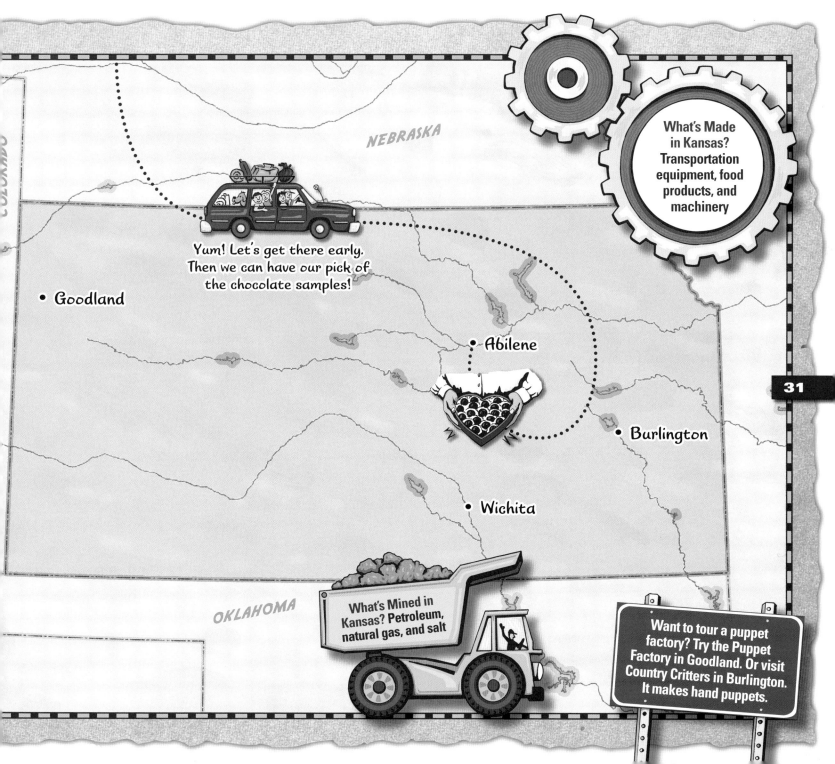

NEBRASKA

COLORADO

Yum! Let's get there early.
Then we can have our pick of
the chocolate samples!

• Goodland

• Abilene

• Burlington

• Wichita

OKLAHOMA

What's Made in Kansas? Transportation equipment, food products, and machinery

What's Mined in Kansas? Petroleum, natural gas, and salt

Want to tour a puppet factory? Try the Puppet Factory in Goodland. Or visit Country Critters in Burlington. It makes hand puppets.

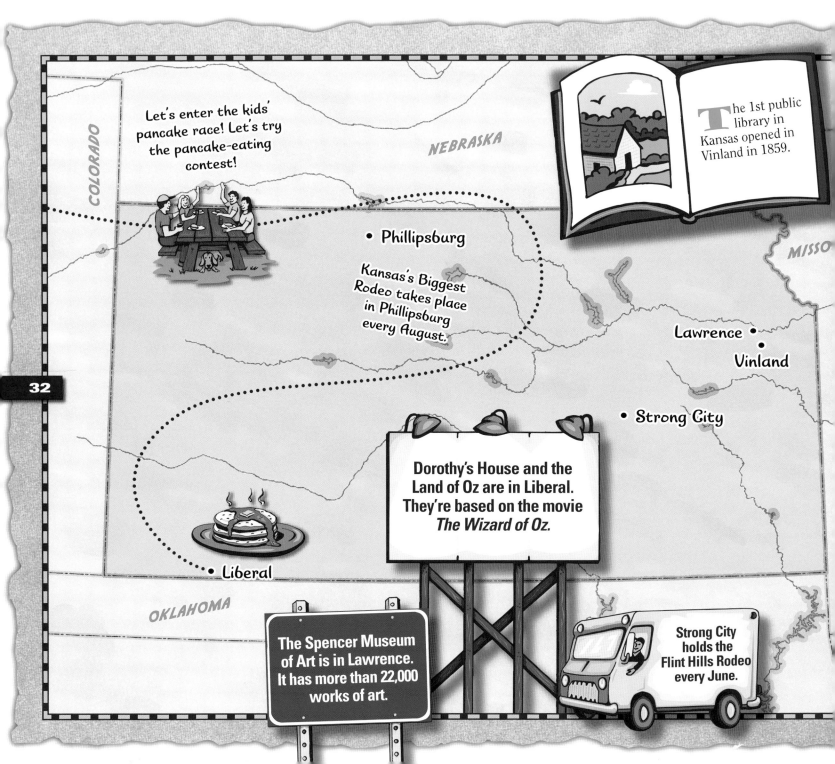

Let's enter the kids' pancake race! Let's try the pancake-eating contest!

NEBRASKA

COLORADO

The 1st public library in Kansas opened in Vinland in 1859.

• Phillipsburg

Kansas's Biggest Rodeo takes place in Phillipsburg every August.

MISSO

Lawrence •
• Vinland

• Strong City

Dorothy's House and the Land of Oz are in Liberal. They're based on the movie *The Wizard of Oz.*

• Liberal

OKLAHOMA

The Spencer Museum of Art is in Lawrence. It has more than 22,000 works of art.

Strong City holds the Flint Hills Rodeo every June.

Racing with Pancakes in Liberal

Ride 'em, cowboy! Rodeos are popular sporting events in Kansas.

Women are racing down the street. Each one's carrying a skillet. They're flipping pancakes while they run!

You're watching the **International** Pancake Race in Liberal. Why is it international? Because women are also racing in Olney, England. Pancake flippers race in both towns at once!

Kansas has lots of fun events. Many cities have rodeos or Wild West festivals. Some events celebrate pioneer days.

There are several places to enjoy nature. Some people like watching birds in wildlife areas. Others enjoy hiking or horseback riding. The state's many lakes are popular, too. People use them for boating, swimming, and fishing.

Kansas Day is January 29. It's a statewide holiday. It celebrates Kansas's statehood date, or birthday!

Kansas State University also has a butterfly conservatory.

Creepy-Crawlies at the Insect Zoo

Would you like to pet a tarantula? Want a cockroach to crawl up your arm? Then stop by the Insect Zoo! It's at Kansas State University in Manhattan.

This is a great zoo for bug lovers. There's a lot of bug stuff to explore. One area is the bug petting zoo. You can hold and pet bugs there. Another area has a beehive. You'll watch the bees eating and even dancing!

One display keeps things dark. There you'll see what bugs do at night. It's all pretty amazing—if you like bugs!

Want to get up close and personal with a tarantula? Visit the Insect Zoo in Manhattan!

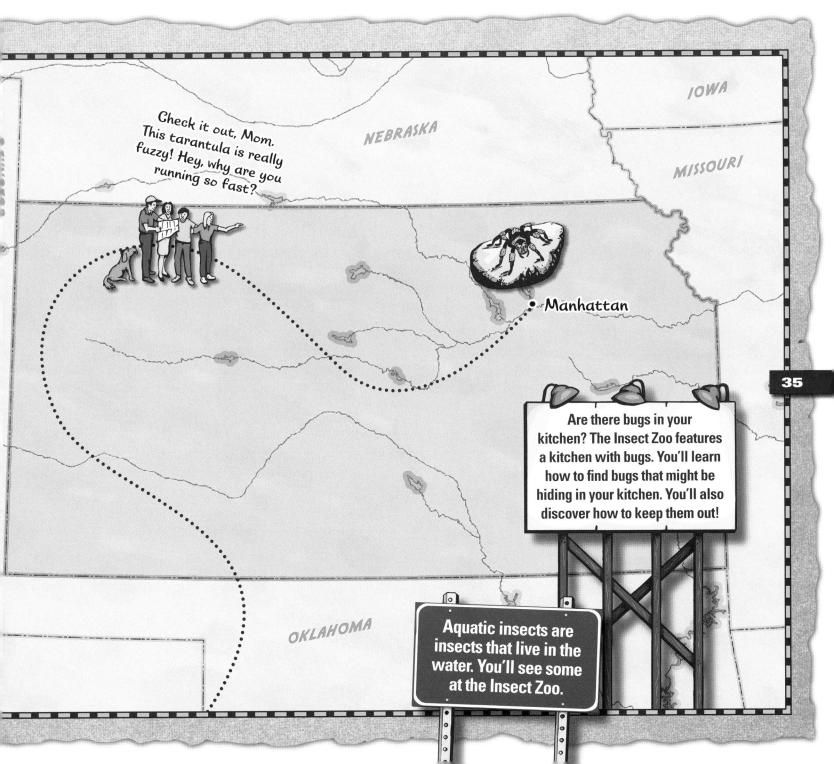

Check it out, Mom. This tarantula is really fuzzy! Hey, why are you running so fast?

NEBRASKA

IOWA

MISSOURI

• Manhattan

Are there bugs in your kitchen? The Insect Zoo features a kitchen with bugs. You'll learn how to find bugs that might be hiding in your kitchen. You'll also discover how to keep them out!

Aquatic insects are insects that live in the water. You'll see some at the Insect Zoo.

OKLAHOMA

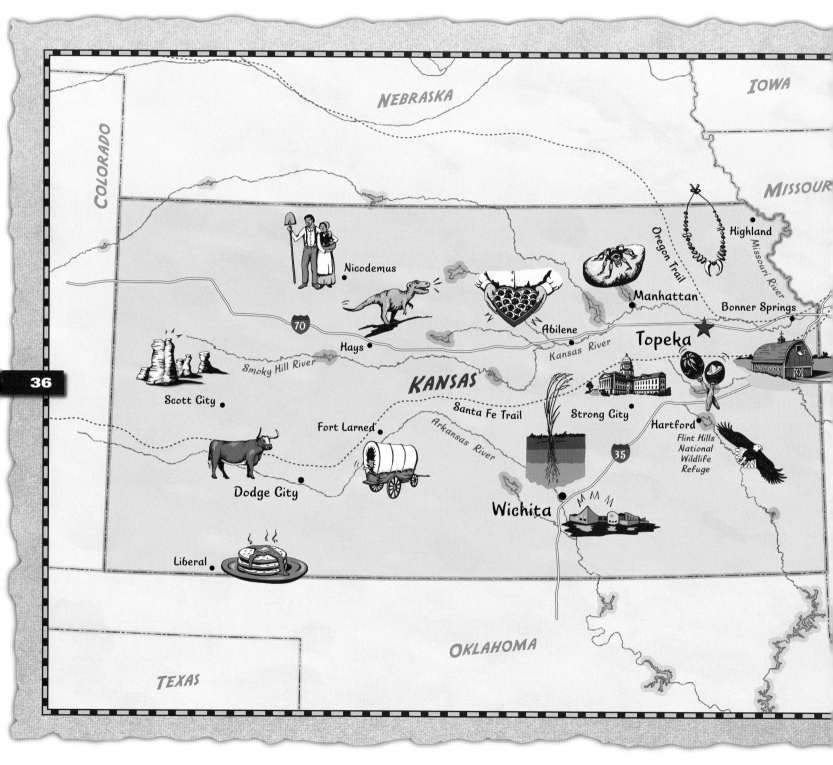

NEBRASKA

IOWA

COLORADO

MISSOURI

Nicodemus

Highland

Oregon Trail

Missouri River

Manhattan

Bonner Springs

70

Hays

Abilene

Topeka

Kansas River

Smoky Hill River

KANSAS

Scott City

Santa Fe Trail

Strong City

Hartford

Fort Larned

Arkansas River

Flint Hills
National
Wildlife
Refuge

35

Dodge City

Wichita

Liberal

OKLAHOMA

TEXAS

OUR TRIP

We visited many amazing places on our trip! We also met a lot of interesting people along the way. Look at the map on the left. Use your finger to trace all the places we have been.

What is Kansas's largest lake? See page 6 for the answer.

When did the fish-within-a-fish live? Page 12 has the answer.

When did Kansas open for white settlement? See page 16 for the answer.

Who helped found Nicodemus? Look on page 19 for the answer.

Where is the Old Cowtown Museum located? Page 21 has the answer.

Why did a stone fence once surround the capitol? Turn to page 26 for the answer.

Which U.S. president grew up in Abilene? Look on page 27 and find out!

When is Kansas Day? Turn to page 33 for the answer.

That was a great trip! We have traveled all over Kansas! There are a few places that we didn't have time for, though. Next time, we plan to visit the Eisenhower Presidential Center in Abilene. We can see the home of the 34th U.S. president! The Center also features a museum and library.

More Places to Visit in Kansas

WORDS TO KNOW

conservatory (kuhn-SUR-vuh-tor-ee) a large, light-filled space for growing flowers and other plants

cultures (KUHL-churz) the customs, beliefs, and ways of life among different groups of people

descendants (di-SEND-uhnts) children, grandchildren, great-grandchildren, and so on

ethnic (ETH-nik) having to do with a person's race or nationality

fossil (FOSS-uhl) the hardened remains of a plant or animal

Hispanic (hiss-PAN-ik) relating to people with roots in Spanish-speaking lands

international (in-tur-NASH-uh-nuhl) involving more than 1 country

jalapeño (ha-la-PAY-nyoh) a very hot pepper

pioneers (pye-uh-NEERZ) the 1st people to move into an unsettled region

reservations (rez-ur-VAY-shuhnz) lands set aside for use by American Indians

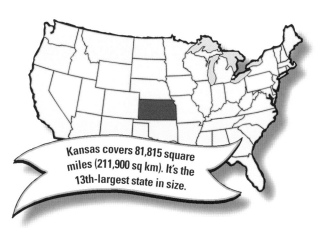

Kansas covers 81,815 square miles (211,900 sq km). It's the 13th-largest state in size.

STATE SYMBOLS

State amphibian: Barred tiger salamander

State animal: American buffalo (bison)

State bird: Western meadowlark

State flower: Sunflower

State insect: Honeybee

State reptile: Ornate box turtle

State soil: Harney silt loam

State tree: Cottonwood

State flag

State seal

STATE SONG

"Home on the Range"

Words by Dr. Brewster Higley, music by Daniel Kelly

Oh, give me a home where the buffalo roam,
Where the deer and the antelope play,
Where seldom is heard a discouraging word
And the sky is not clouded all day.

Chorus:
A home, a home where the deer and the antelope play,
Where seldom is heard a discouraging word
And the sky is not clouded all day.

Oh, give me a land where the bright diamond sand
Throws its light from the glittering stream
Where glideth along the graceful white swan,
Like the maid in her heavenly dreams.

Oh, give me the gale of the Solomon vale,
Where life streams with buoyancy flow;
On the banks of the Beaver, where seldom if ever
Any poisonous herbage doth grow.

How often at night, when the heavens were bright
With the light of the glittering stars,
Have I stood here amazed and asked as I gazed
If their glory exceeds that of ours.

I love the wild flowers in this bright land of ours;
I love too the wild curlew's shrill scream
The bluffs and white rocks and antelope flocks
That graze on the mountains so green.

The air is so pure and the breezes so fine,
The zephyrs so balmy and light,
I would not exchange my home here to range
Forever in azure so bright.

FAMOUS PEOPLE

Bosin, Black Bear (1921–1980), Native American artist

Brooks, Gwendolyn (1917–2000), poet

Chamberlain, Wilt (1936–1999), basketball player

Chrysler, Walter P. (1875–1940), automobile manufacturer

Dole, Bob (1923–), senator

Earhart, Amelia (1897–1937), aviator

Earp, Wyatt (1848–1929), lawman

Eisenhower, Dwight D. (1890–1969), 34th U.S. president

Hopper, Dennis (1936–), actor

Hughes, Langston (1902–1967), poet and author

Inge, William (1913–1973), playwright

Johnson, Walter Perry (1887–1946), baseball player

Keaton, Buster (1895–1966), comedic actor

Kelly, Emmett (1898–1979), clown

Kenton, Stan (1911–1979), jazz musician

Lehrer, Jim (1934–), journalist

Martin, Bill, Jr. (1916–2004), children's author

McDaniel, Hattie (1895–1952), actor

Pitts, Zasu (1894–1963), actor

Sanders, Barry (1968–), football player

TO FIND OUT MORE

At the Library
Cooper, Floyd. *Coming Home: From the Life of Langston Hughes.* New York: Philomel Books, 1994.

Fradin, Dennis Brindell, and Judith Bloom Fradin. *Kansas.* Chicago: Children's Press, 1995.

Garretson, Jerri. *Kansas Katie: A Sunflower Tale.* Manhattan, Kan.: Ravenstone Press, 2000.

Scillian, Devin S., Corey Scillian, and Doug Bowles (illustrator). *S Is for Sunflower: A Kansas Alphabet.* Chelsea, Mich.: Sleeping Bear Press, 2004.

On the Web
Visit our home page for lots of links about Kansas: *http://www.childsworld.com/links*

Note to Parents, Teachers, and Librarians: We routinely verify our Web links to make sure they are safe, active sites—so encourage your readers to check them out!

Places to Visit or Contact
Kansas Department of Travel and Tourism
700 SW Harrison, Suite 1300
Topeka, KS 66603
800/252-6727
For more information about traveling in Kansas

Kansas State Historical Society
6425 SW Sixth Avenue
Topeka, KS 66615
785/272-8681
For more information about the history of Kansas

INDEX

40

Bye, Sunflower State.
We had a great time.
We'll come back soon!

20th Century Lives

SPORTS HEROES

Jane Bingham

PowerKiDS
press.

New York

Published in 2011 by The Rosen Publishing Group Inc.
29 East 21st Street, New York, NY 10010

Copyright © 2011 Wayland/
The Rosen Publishing Group, Inc.

First Edition

Designer Jason Billin
Editor Nicola Edwards
Picture Researcher: Louise Edgeworth

Library of Congress Cataloging-in-Publication Data

Bingham, Jane.
Sports heroes / by Jane Bingham. — 1st ed.
p. cm. — (20th century lives)
Includes index.
ISBN 978-1-4488-3294-1 (library binding)
1. Athletes—Biography—Juvenile literature. I. Title.
GV697.A1B485 2011
796.0922—dc22
[B]
2010024104

Photographs:
Cover: PA Photos/PA Archive; title page: Rex Features: CSU Archives/Everett Collection, Alamy: John Fryer p. 20, The Photolibrary Wales p. 21, Aflo Photo Agency/Alamy p. 27; Corbis: Bettman p. 6, p. 7, p. 11, p. 15 & p. 26. George Tiedemann/GT Images p. 13, Schlegelmilch p. 18, Dimitri Lundt/TempSport p. 22; Getty Images: Shaun Botterill/Allsport p. 2 & p. 17, Allsport/Hulton Archive p. 8, Fox Photos p. 9, Frederick M Brown p. 16, David Cannon p. 24, Bob Thomas p. 28, Jerry Wachter/NBAE via Getty Images p. 29; PA Photos: Panoramic p. 4 & p. 12, Gareth Copley/PA Archive p. 5, PA Archive p. 14, Neal Simpson/Empics Sport p. 23, Presse Sports p. 25; Rex Features: CSU Archives/Everett Collection p. 1 & p. 10, Sipa Press p. 19.

Manufactured in China
CPSIA Compliance Information: Batch #WAW1102PK: For Further Information
contact Rosen Publishing, New York, New York at 1-800-237-9932

Contents

The Brazilian soccer player, Pelé, celebrates after scoring his thousandth goal. This famous goal is sometimes known as O Milésimo and was scored in Brazil's Maracanã Stadium in 1969.

Pelé dedicated his thousandth goal to the poor children of Brazil. Many sports heroes have used their fame, skill, and wealth to help others.

What Makes a Sports Hero?

When soccer legend Pelé scored his thousandth goal, people all over the world went wild. They knew that they were watching one of the most outstanding athletes of all time. Since he was a teenager, Pelé had astonished everyone who saw him play with his skill, speed, and style.

Sports heroes like Pelé make our lives more exciting. They provide an inspiring example to other athletes. They also demonstrate that it is possible to achieve some truly extraordinary feats.

What Does It Take?

All sports heroes have incredible skills. But simply being skillful is not enough. In order to be the best, athletes need to train incredibly hard, devoting most of their time and energy to practicing their sport.

In all sports, people risk painful injuries. They can also face some serious disappointments and setbacks. Yet, despite these obstacles, sports heroes do not give up. They keep trying to achieve the best they possibly can.

Twentieth-Century Sports

The 16 men and women featured in this book are some of the greatest names in twentieth-century sports. They represent a wide range of sports and nationalities. They also reflect the ways that sports have changed over the last hundred years.

In the early twentieth century, many sports heroes were amateurs, and even professionals were not very well paid, but, by the 1980s, most sports had

Tanni Grey-Thompson is a leading wheelchair athlete from Wales. She has competed in five Paralympics, winning 16 medals, including 11 golds. The idea of holding a Paralympic Games for disabled athletes had its origins in 1948, and the first Olympic-style event took place in Rome in 1960.

become dominated by professionals. Leading sportsmen and women had become celebrities, who could expect to earn vast sums of money. At the same time, the number of women competitors grew very fast, and opportunities increased for disabled athletes.

A Lasting Legacy

The sports heroes of the twentieth century have left a great legacy for the future. Some of them have set records that have not yet been matched. Some have taken their sport in fresh directions and attracted new audiences. Most important of all, they have all provided an inspiring example to the athletes who have come after them.

"We all have dreams. But in order to make dreams come into reality, it takes an awful lot of determination, dedication, self-discipline, and effort." *Jesse Owens*

Babe Rut[h]

One of the Greatest-Ever Baseball Players

"You just can't beat the person who never gives up."

Babe Ruth

A Tough Childhood

Babe Ruth came from a very poor family in the town of Baltimore, Maryland. His father, George Herman Ruth, Sr., ran a series of bars. His busy job left him with little time to spend with his young family. Babe's mother, Kate Schamberger-Ruth, was sick with tuberculosis (a serious lung disease). She died when Babe was a teenager. Of his seven brothers and sisters, only one sister, Marnie, survived to be an adult.

When Babe was seven years old, his father sent him to St. Mary's Industrial School for boys, a very tough boarding school run by Catholic priests. He stayed there for the next 12 years, and only visited his family for special occasions.

A Life-Changing Influence

Babe found it hard to deal with the strict environment of the school and was criticized for his bad behavior. However, Brother Matthias, the school's Prefect of Discipline, was to have a very positive effect on Babe's behavior. The priest became a father figure for Babe, making sure that he learned to read and write, and coaching him in baseball. Babe developed a great talent for the game, both as a left-handed pitcher and as a powerful hitter. He played for the school team, in a variety of positions but most often as catcher.

Name George Herman Ruth, Jr.

Nickname Babe Ruth. He was given his nickname when he started playing professional baseball at 19.

Born February 6, 1895, in Baltimore, Maryland

Died August 16, 1948

Personal Life He married twice and had two daughters.

High Point In 1927, he became the first baseball player to hit 60 home runs in one season.

Low Point In 1917, he punched an umpire and was suspended for ten games.

Surprising Fact When he was sick with stomach problems in 1925, it was such big news that journalists called it "the bellyache that was heard all over the world."

From Baltimore to Boston

At the age of 19, Babe's talent was noticed by a scout and he was chosen to play for the Baltimore Orioles. Less than six months later, he was sold to the Boston Red Sox. He played for the Red Sox for the next five years, and became famous for his fast pitching and his amazing swing. Babe could hit the ball harder and faster than anyone had done before.

Yankees' Superstar

In 1919, Babe Ruth joined the New York Yankees. His career for the Yankees lasted 15 years and consisted of over 2,000 games. In this period, he set many baseball records. For example, in 1927, he became the first player to achieve 60 home runs (running all the way around the baseball diamond without stopping) within a single season. This record stayed unbroken for 34 years.

With Babe Ruth as the star attraction in the team, the number of Yankees fans grew. In 1923, the club built the famous Yankee Stadium, which became known as "the house that Babe built."

Later Years

In 1935, the 40-year-old Babe transferred to the Boston Braves, but the following year he announced his retirement. By that time, his career total of 714 home runs was a world record, and was 336 more than the total of the next player.

After he retired, Babe became a radio star, often hosting baseball quiz shows. He also had made several appearances in movies, usually playing himself. He died from cancer at the age of 53.

Babe Ruth, playing for the Yankees, watches a ball that he has just hit sail toward the outfield wall. He was famous for his powerful swing.

Twentieth-Century Legacy

Babe Ruth turned baseball into a high-scoring power sport, and made it popular all over the world. He was one of the first international sports stars. People in many countries knew his name and a popular candy bar was named after him.

Donald Bradman

Cricket's Greatest-Ever Batsman

"I was never coached; I was never told how to hold a bat."

Donald Bradman

Early Practice

Don Bradman spent his childhood in Bowral, a small country town in New South Wales, Australia. He was the youngest of five children, and spent a lot of his childhood playing alone.

As a young boy, Don invented a solo cricket game, using a stump of wood to hit a golf ball against a curved brick wall, and then trying to hit the ball again when it bounced off the wall. This early practice helped him to develop excellent timing and incredibly fast reactions.

A Brilliant Start

At the age of 14, Don went to work at a real estate office, but he also played cricket for Bowral, and in 1926, he was selected for the state team of New South Wales. In his very first state match, at 19 years old, he achieved a century (100 runs).

Breaking Records

In the following year, he began playing in Test matches for Australia. Before he was 22, he had set many batting records, some of which are still unbeaten today. During this time, Don gained a reputation for a very exciting batting style, sometimes using strokes that reminded the spectators of golf or tennis.

Name Sir Donald George Bradman

Nickname The Don

Born August 27, 1908 in Cootamundra, New South Wales, Australia

Died February 25, 2001

Personal Life He married in 1932 and had two sons and a daughter.

High Point In a match in 1930, he scored an astonishing 974 runs, a record that is still unbeaten.

Low Point In his last Test match, in 1948, he was bowled out on the second ball.

Surprising Fact He learned to play cricket on concrete wickets covered with matting, and did not bat and run on grass until he was 18.

Great Achievements

Altogether, Don played for Australia for 20 years, but in 1934, he missed a year of play when he became very sick with appendicitis. However, he soon returned to top form. In the third Test match against England in 1937, he made 270 runs. This score has been rated as the greatest innings of all time.

During World War II (1939–1945), international cricket stopped, but after the war, Don played for Australia for three more years, before retiring in 1948 at the age of 40. At the end of his career, he had achieved an average in Test cricket matches of 99.94 runs, over 40 runs more than anyone has ever managed since.

Private Life

Away from the cricket pitch, Don lived a quiet life in a small house in Adelaide. He and his wife Jessie were married for 65 years. The family suffered several tragedies. Don and Jessie's first son died as a baby, their second son caught polio and was paralyzed for a year, and their daughter was born with cerebral palsy (a condition that causes severe paralysis).

In 1949, Don was knighted by Queen Elizabeth II. He was the first cricketer to be honored in this way for his services to the sport.

Spectators at the Headingly ground in Leeds, UK, applaud Donald Bradman as he comes out to bat for Australia during a Test match in 1938.

Twentieth-Century Legacy

Donald Bradman is Australia's greatest sports hero. In 2001, the Australian prime minister called him the "greatest living Australian." With his exciting, attacking style, Bradman drew record crowds to watch cricket matches. He has inspired generations of cricketers. The former captain of the Australian cricket team, Steve Waugh, has described Bradman as "a once-in-a-lifetime player."

Jesse Owens

One of the First Great U.S. Athletes

"We all have dreams. But in order to make dreams come into reality, it takes an awful lot of determination, dedication, self-discipline, and effort."

Jesse Owens

A Young Athlete

Jesse Owens grew up in the Oakville community of African Americans, close to Cleveland, Alabama. His family was poor and Jesse had to take a variety of jobs, such as delivering groceries and repairing shoes. At school, he was encouraged to join the running team. He practiced early in the morning, so he could work after school. He went on to become a champion athlete in track and field events, such as the sprint and the long jump.

Record Beater

When he was 22, Jesse won a place at Ohio State University. As a member of the university athletics team, he competed in national competitions, winning many medals. In one competition in Ann Arbor, Michigan, in 1935, Jesse managed a remarkable set of achievements. He equalled the world record for the 100-yard (91-meter) sprint, and set world records in the long jump, the 220-yard (201.2-m) sprint, and the low hurdles events.

Name James Cleveland Owens

Nickname Jesse. He was called Jesse at school, when he said his name was "J.C."

Born September 12, 1913, in Oakville, Alabama

Died March 31, 1980

Personal Life Jesse married in 1935 and he had three daughters.

High Point In 1936, he became the first American to win four Olympic gold medals in track and field events.

Low Point After Jesse's Olympic victories, Adolf Hitler, the Chancellor of Germany, did not shake his hand, and President F. D. Roosevelt failed to congratulate him. Jesse was very upset about this obvious racism.

Surprising Fact As an Olympic hero, Jesse was given a party in a New York hotel, but he was not allowed to ride in the same elevator as his white guests.

Jesse Owens astonished the crowds at the Berlin Olympics with his skill, speed, and style. He is shown here performing the long jump.

An Olympic Hero

The 1936 Olympic Games were run by Adolf Hitler's Nazi Party. Hitler had planned to use the Olympics to show that German athletes were the best, but during the Games, it was Jesse Owens who really stunned the crowds. He won the 100-meter sprint, the long jump, and the 200-meter sprint. He was also part of the U.S. team that won the 100-meter relay race. Hitler was furious, and said that black athletes should be disqualified in the future. However, many German people saw Jesse as a hero.

After the Olympics

Jesse did not compete in any more major events. In that era, it was very hard for black people to be accepted in white society. For the next 20 years, he struggled to earn a living. Then, in the 1960s, Jesse began a career as a speaker. He traveled the world encouraging people to achieve their best.

Twentieth-Century Legacy

At the Berlin Olympics, Jesse showed the world what an African-American athlete could achieve. He has become a hero for black competitors in all sports. Following his death in 1980, the Jesse Owens Foundation was set up in Ohio to encourage young people to develop their full potential.

Pelé
Greatest Soccer Player of All Time

"Enthusiasm is everything.
It must be taut and vibrating
like a guitar string."

Pelé

A Poor Childhood

Pelé's family lived in the town of Bauru, Brazil. His father was a soccer player who had to retire early, and he coached his son. The family was very poor, and Pelé earned extra money as a shoeshine boy. When he was young, his family could not afford a proper soccer ball for Pelé to practice with, so he used a grapefruit or a sock stuffed with newspaper.

By the time he reached his teens, Pelé had developed amazing skills at tackling and passing, taking headers, and scoring goals. At 15 years old, he was picked for the Santos FC junior team and after just one season he joined the senior team.

A Brilliant Career

In his first season playing for Santos, the 16-year-old Pelé was the top scorer in the Brazilian league. In the following year, at the age of 17, he became the youngest player ever to play in a World Cup Final, scoring two goals for Brazil. After the World Cup, European clubs offered massive fees to sign the young player, but the government of Brazil declared Pelé an "official national treasure" to prevent him being signed up by another country.

Pelé played for Santos until 1974 and was Brazil's star player in a team that contained many talented members. He played as an inside forward and a striker and in the vital playmaker position,

Name Edison Arantes do Nascimento
Nickname Pelé. He was given this nickname by friends at school.
Born October 23, 1940, in Três Corações, Brazil
Personal Life He has been married twice and has seven children.
High Point On November 19, 1969, Pelé scored his thousandth goal in all competitions. He dedicated it to the poor children of Brazil.
Low Point In the 1962 World Cup, Pelé was injured in the second round so he could not play in the final match.
Surprising Fact In Nigeria in 1968, a two-day truce was declared in the war with Biafra so that both sides could watch Pelé play.

controlling his team's attacking play. In his 22-year career, Pelé scored 1,281 goals and was the only soccer player to play in three World Cup winning teams. He became an international soccer legend,

For three years in the 1970s, the American public had the chance to see Pelé in action, playing for the New York Cosmos. He is shown here in a game against the Washington Diplomats.

famous for his elegant playing style, his astonishing speed, and his remarkable ball control.

Later Life

In 1975, Pelé signed up with the New York Cosmos, and played three seasons for them, helping to raise American interest in soccer. Since his retirement from soccer in 1977, he has run businesses, performed in movies, and campaigned on a range of issues, including ecology and the environment.

Twentieth-Century Legacy

Pelé has inspired generations of young soccer players everywhere, but especially in the less-developed countries of the world. He has shown the world what a beautiful game soccer can be when it is played with such incredible skill.

Muhammad Ali

Three-Time Heavyweight Boxing World Champion

"Float like a butterfly,
sting like a bee."

Muhammad Ali

Name Muhammad Ali

Original Name Cassius Marcellus Clay, Jr. Ali changed his name in 1964 when he converted to the Muslim religion.

Born January 17, 1942, in Louisville, Kentucky

Personal Life He has been married four times and has seven daughters and two sons.

High Point In 1974, Ali won a surprise victory against George Foreman, in a thrilling fight in Zaire, known as "the rumble in the jungle."

Low Point In 1975, he fought an exhibition match against Antonio Inoki, who concentrated his attack on Ali's legs. The result was a draw, but Ali's legs were permanently weakened.

Surprising Fact The singer Frank Sinatra was so anxious to see the Ali-Frazier fight in 1971 that he agreed to photograph the fight for *Match* magazine.

Starting Young

Until he was 22, Muhammad Ali was named Cassius Clay. He grew up in Louisville, Kentucky, where his father was a sign painter and his mother worked as a cleaner. At the age of 12, he started learning to box and was soon winning amateur titles.

In 1960, at the age of 18, Ali won the Olympic Light Heavyweight gold medal. Following this triumph, he returned to Louisville to begin his professional career. At the end of his time as an amateur, he had won a hundred fights and lost only five.

Religion and War

Between 1960 and 1963, Ali fought 19 matches and won them all. He gained a reputation as a very stylish fighter, who was incredibly light on his feet and speedy with his punches. At the same time, he became famous for his self-confidence, bragging before matches and taunting his opponents.

In 1964, Ali had his first professional title fight, beating Sonny Liston to become the World Heavyweight Boxing Champion. Later that year, he announced his conversion to Islam and changed his name to Muhammad Ali. In 1967, he refused to

In 1965, Muhammad Ali fought Sonny Liston to defend his title as World Heavyweight Champion. Ali knocked Liston out after one minute in the first round. In this photograph, Liston is shown struggling to recover, but soon after this, the referee decided that Ali had won the fight.

join the U.S. army and fight in the Vietnam War. As a result of this, he was put on trial and banned from professional boxing.

Wins and Losses

In 1970, Ali was allowed to fight again. A year later, he was defeated by Joe Frazier in a fight promoted as "the fight of the century." However, in 1974, he regained his World Heavyweight title when he beat George Foreman. Ali lost his title in February 1978, when he was beaten by Leon Spinks, but seven months later, he won the title back from Spinks.

Later Life

In 1979, Ali retired from professional boxing. Since then he has campaigned for many causes, especially world peace, understanding, and respect. In 1984, he was diagnosed with Parkinson's Disease (a condition that makes people shake uncontrollably) but he has continued with his work as an activist.

Twentieth-Century Legacy

Through his self-promotion and his skill in the ring, Ali turned boxing into a very popular spectator sport. He is the world's most famous African-American sports personality and he has helped to inspire many black athletes.

15

Steffi Graf

The Greatest Female Tennis Player of the Twentieth Century

"As long as I can focus on enjoying what I'm doing, having fun, I know I'll play well."

Steffi Graf

Early Promise

Steffi Graf grew up in the town of Mannheim, Germany. She was taught to play tennis by her father, who showed her how to swing a racket when she was only three. By the time she was four, she was practicing on a court and she played in her first tournament when she was five. She soon began winning junior championships, and in 1982, at 13 years old, she played in her first adult professional tennis tournament.

Rising Through the Ranks

During her early years as a young professional player, Steffi's father made sure that she did not "burn out" by playing too many matches. He also insisted that she should concentrate on practicing her tennis rather than attending social events. In her first year in professional tennis, Steffi was ranked as world number 124. Within three years, she had risen to world number 6, at the age of 16.

Grand Slams

In 1986, Steffi won her first World Tennis Association tournament, beating Chris Evert. The following year, she won several tournaments and in 1988, she

Name Stefanie Maria Graf

Nickname Steffi

Born June 14, 1969 in Mannheim, Germany

Personal Life She is married to the U.S. tennis champion, André Agassi, and has a son and a daughter.

High Point In 1988, Steffi won an Olympic gold medal for singles tennis, just one week after achieving the "Calendar Year Grand Slam" (see main text). Journalists called it the "Golden Slam."

Low Point In 1995, she was accused of not paying enough tax. Her father, who had managed her money, went to jail for two years and Steffi had to pay a large fine.

Surprising Fact Steffi's husband, André Agassi, claims he had been secretly pining for her since 1990. They got married in 2001.

achieved a "Calendar Year Grand Slam," winning all four "Grand Slam" titles (the Australian Open, the French Open, Wimbledon, and the U.S. Open).

She proved herself to be equally skillful on all playing surfaces, and she became famous for her hard-hitting style. Over the next two years, she continued to win many Grand Slam titles, but 1991–1992 was a difficult period because she suffered illness and injuries.

Steffi Graf is famous for her powerful backhand strokes. She is shown here in action in the 1996 U.S. Open Tennis Championships semifinals. Steffi went on to win the competition.

Injuries and Achievements

From 1993 to 1996, Steffi returned to winning form, but she also suffered from serious back problems, sometimes having to wear a brace between matches. An injured knee meant that she could not take part in the Summer Olympics of 1996 and she missed many matches over the next two years due to injury.

Retirement and Beyond

In 1999, Steffi announced her retirement from international tennis, even though she was still ranked number three in the world. This made her the highest-ranked player to announce retirement from the sport since computerized records began. During her career, she had won an astonishing total of 22 Grand Slam singles titles.

Steffi now supports several charities, including the Worldwide Fund for Nature, for which she is an international ambassador. She has founded a youth tennis center in Germany and a charity called Children for Tomorrow that supports children whose lives have been damaged by war.

Twentieth-Century Legacy

Steffi Graf demonstrated that a female tennis player could show great stamina, speed, and skill on all playing surfaces. She also proved that it was possible for a woman player to have a very strong service. Her serve could reach speeds of 110 mph (180 km/h).

Ayrton Senna

Formula One Champion and Brazilian National Hero

"Each driver has his limit. My limit is a little bit further than others."

Ayrton Senna

Starting Young

Ayrton Senna was the son of a wealthy Brazilian landowner. As a boy he was very interested in the sport of kart racing and, at the age of 17, he won the South American Kart Championship. By the time he reached his twenties, Ayrton had become more interested in motor racing. In 1981, he moved to the UK to take up a career as a racing driver.

Formula One

In the UK, Ayrton quickly moved up the ranks of motor racing, winning the Formula Three championship in 1983. In the following year, he began Formula One racing, as a member of the Toleman team. In 1985, he moved to the Lotus-Renault team and over the next three seasons, he won a total of six Grand Prix races.

In 1988, Ayrton joined the McLaren-Honda team, where he developed a rivalry with his teammate, Alain Prost. In the same year, he and Prost won 15 out of the 16 Grand Prix races of the season, and Ayrton won his first Formula One World Championship title (awarded to the driver with the highest number of points in the season). He

Name Ayrton Senna da Silva

Born March 21, 1960, in Sao Paolo, Brazil

Died May 1, 1994

Personal Life Ayrton was a devout Christian who secretly donated large amounts of his winnings to poor Brazilian children.

High Point In 1991, at Suzuka, in Japan, Ayrton realized he would win the World Championship even if he came second, so he slowed down to allow Gerhard Berger, his McLaren teammate, to win.

Low Point In 1989, the rivalry between Ayrton and Alain Prost led to a collision on the track at Suzuka. Ayrton went on to win the race, but he was disqualified and given a heavy fine.

Surprising Fact Ayrton began racing when he took over a gift rejected by his older sister—a go-kart with a lawn-mower engine.

won the Championship again in 1990 and 1991. In 1992, the performance of the McLaren-Honda team began to decline, and in 1994, Ayrton signed up with the Williams-Renault team.

This photograph shows Ayrton Senna racing for the Honda-McLaren team in 1991, three years before his fatal accident at the age of 34.

Danger at San Marino

Ayrton's third race with his new team was the San Marino Grand Prix, held at Imola in Italy. On the day before the race, Roland Ratzenberger, an Austrian driver, was killed while he was practicing on the track. Ayrton was very upset by Ratzenberger's death and he held a meeting with his fellow drivers. In the meeting, Ayrton volunteered to lead a group to increase safety in Formula One racing.

A Fatal Accident

Ayrton took the lead in the race, but on the seventh lap, his car spun out of control and crashed into a concrete barrier. He was airlifted to the hospital where he was declared dead. In Brazil, the government announced three days of national mourning and more than a million people attended his burial.

Twentieth-Century Legacy

Ayrton's death on the track led to many improvements in motor racing safety. Since 1994, most tracks have been redesigned to make them safer, and better crash barriers have been installed. Ayrton is also remembered in the Insituto Ayrton Senna. After he died, it was discovered that he had donated millions of dollars to help poor children in Brazil, and the Instituto continues this work.

Tanni Grey-Thompson

Paralympian Wheelchair Athlete

"I like pushing myself to the limit."

Tanni Grey-Thompson

Early Life

Tanni Grey-Thompson comes from Cardiff, Wales, in the UK. She was born with spina bifida, a medical condition in which the spine is not properly formed. This meant she was paralyzed from the waist down. As a small girl she had to wear braces to support her legs, and when she was seven, she began to use a wheelchair. However, her disability did not stop her from trying out sports. While she was at school, she especially enjoyed swimming, archery, and horseback-riding.

Wheelchair Racer

At the age of 13, Tanni started wheelchair racing, and two years later, she won the 100-meter race at the Junior National Wheelchair Games. When she was 18, she was selected for the British Wheelchair Racing Squad. In 1988, at the age of 19, Tanni won a bronze medal at the Seoul Paralympics. Over the next few years, she had some major back surgery but was also able to study for a degree in politics at Loughborough University and keep up her training as a wheelchair racer.

Great Achievements

At the Barcelona Paralympics in 1992, Tanni won four gold medals in the 100-, 200-, 400-, and 800-meter races. Later the same year, she won her first

Name Dame Carys Davina Grey-Thompson

Nickname Tanni. When her older sister first saw baby Carys, she called her "Tiny," which she pronounced as "Tanni."

Born July 26, 1969 in Cardiff, Wales

Personal Life In 1999, Tanni married Ian Thompson, who is also a wheelchair athlete. They have one daughter.

High Point Winning four gold medals at the Sydney Paralympics in 2000.

Low Point In 1989, the year after her first Paralympics, Tanni had to miss a year of sports while she had surgery on her spine.

Surprising Fact Tanni's racing chair is made to fit her exactly. She can only fit into it when she is wearing her lycra racing suit.

London Wheelchair Marathon. Since then, she has won the Marathon five more times, and has competed in five Paralympics, winning 16 medals, including 11 golds.

In 2005, Tanni was made a Dame Commander of the Order of the British Empire in recognition of her outstanding services to sports. Two years later, she retired from athletics at the age of 35, but she still plays a very active part in promoting sports in the UK.

Antidrug Campaigner

Tanni is a strong advocate of strict drug tests for athletes. In 2008, she was asked to investigate government policies on drugs in sports. Her report recommended that the UK government should make more efforts to prevent the use of performance-enhancing drugs by athletes.

Tanni Grey-Thompson competes in the 800-meter race during the Welsh Senior Championship and Cardiff Centenary Games. The Games were held in 2005 at the Leckwith Stadium in Tanni's home city of Cardiff, in the UK.

Twentieth-Century Legacy

During her career, Tanni showed what could be achieved through determination and self-belief. She is an inspiration to all athletes, and especially to those with disabilities. She is also helping to make sports free from drugs.

Jonah Lomu

First Global Superstar of Rugby Union

"I think everyone has a pure, natural talent. The responsibility on the individual is to grow with it and enhance it."

Jonah Lomu

Early Career

Jonah Lomu's family originally came from the island of Tonga, and he grew up in a poor district of Auckland, New Zealand. At school, Jonah excelled in sports and, when he was 14, he was invited to join a team of promising teenagers playing rugby union.

International Star

In 1994, at the age of 19, Jonah played his first international match for the New Zealand All Blacks. In the following year, he took part in the Rugby World Cup, scoring an amazing seven tries in five matches.

On the field, Jonah stood out from all the other players because of his size and strength—he is 6 feet 5 inches (1.96 meters) tall and weighs 265 pounds (120 kg). He could also run extremely fast and had the ability to bulldoze his way through an opposing team's defense.

In 1996, Jonah was a key member of the team that became the first champions of the newly-created

Name Jonah Tali Lomu

Born May 12, 1975, in Auckland, New Zealand

Personal Life Jonah has been married and divorced twice. He lives with his third partner who gave birth to Jonah's first child in 2009.

High Point In 1995, he scored four tries in the World Cup semifinal against England.

Low Point In 2003, Jonah's doctor told him he would end up in a wheelchair if he did not have a kidney transplant soon.

Surprising Fact Each of Jonah's thighs has a circumference of 33 inches—the size of an average man's waist.

Tri Nations Series. This competition was held between the three nations of New Zealand, Australia, and South Africa. Jonah scored in the game against Australia that New Zealand won by 32 points to 25.

Health Problems

Ever since he was a boy, Jonah had fought against extreme tiredness, relying on his incredible willpower to carry him through rugby games. Then, at the end of 1996, the cause of his problems was discovered. He was diagnosed with a rare kidney disease and given emergency treatment in the hospital.

Jonah missed the 1997 Series but he was back playing international rugby later that year. In 1998, he won a gold medal representing New Zealand in the sevens rugby event of the Commonwealth Games, held at Kuala Lumpur in Malaysia.

Over the next few years, Jonah continued to play as much as he could, including his star performance in the World Cup in 1995 (see panel on page 22). However, his kidney disease grew gradually worse and by 2003, he needed kidney dialysis treatment for eight hours a day several times a week.

Recovery, Injury, and Retirement

In 2004, Jonah was given a kidney transplant, and by 2005, he was playing international rugby again. Since then, he has suffered several injuries, and in 2007, he announced his retirement.

Jonah Lomu is a powerfully built athlete who is famous for his speed on the field, but he has had to battle with serious kidney disease. At one stage, he described himself as being "so sick I couldn't even run past a little baby."

Twentieth-Century Legacy

Jonah's massive size and powerful attacking style added an element of drama to rugby union, bringing many new fans to the sport. Jonah has also been an inspiring example to others through his courageous struggle against ill health.

Jack Nicklaus

The Greatest Professional Golfer of All Time

A Young Golfer

Jack Nicklaus was the son of a pharmacist and grew up in the suburb of Upper Arlington, close to Columbus, Ohio. He started playing golf when he was ten years old. In his early teens, he had a mild case of polio (a disease that can leave people partly paralyzed) and began to practice golf very seriously to help himself recover.

When Jack was 16 years old, he won the Ohio State Open Golf Championship, and at the age of 20, he came second in the U.S. Open.

Jack the Champion

In 1962, Jack turned professional, and later that year he won the U.S. Open, starting a long career of championship wins. Between the years 1962 and 1986, he won an amazing total of 18 major championships in 25 seasons. Throughout his long career, he was famous for his long, straight drives.

Later Career

In 1986, at the age of 46, Jack won his sixth Masters Cup victory, becoming the oldest person to win the cup, a record that still stands. Jack finally retired from professional golf in 2005, at the age of 65. He now spends much of his time designing golf courses.

Name Jack William Nicklaus

Nickname The Golden Bear

Born January 21, 1940, in Columbus, Ohio

Personal Life He is married and has five children.

High Point In 1978, he achieved a "career Grand Slam," becoming the only player to have won all four major golf championships three times.

Low Point In 1968 and 1969, Jack did not win an Open, but by 1970, he was playing even better than before.

Eddy Merckx

The Most Successful Cyclist of the Twentieth Century

Early Career

Eddy Merckx was the son of a grocer in Brussels, Belgium. At the age of eight, he was given a second-hand racing bike and, by the time he was 16, he was winning cycle club races. In 1964, he became the world amateur cycling champion and the following year he turned professional.

Riding to Victory

In 1966, the 20-year-old Eddy won the Milan-San Remo race. This was followed by a series of victories, but his major breakthrough came in 1969 when he won the *Tour de France* (the most important road cycling race in the world). In this race, he won the yellow jersey for overall leader, the green jersey for best sprinter, and the red polka-dotted jersey for best climber in the mountains. No other rider has achieved this triple in the *Tour de France*.

Record-Breaker

Between 1968 and 1974, Eddy won a record 11 Grand Tours (the three biggest road races in the cycling word, held in France, Italy, and Spain). In 1972, he broke the record for the longest distance cycled in one hour. His distance of 30.715 miles (49.431 km) remained unbeaten for 12 years. Eddy retired in 1978, at the age of 32.

Name Baron Edouard Louis Joseph Merckx

Born June 17, 1945, in Meensel-Kiezegem, Belgium

Personal Life He is married and has a son and a daughter.

High Point In 1974, Eddy won the *Giro d'Italia*, the *Tour de France*, and the World Championship Road Race to achieve the "Triple Crown" in cycling.

Low Point In 1969, he was involved in an accident when he and his pacer (a cyclist who helps another to keep up a certain speed for part of a race) were forced to fall. The pacer was killed instantly and Eddy suffered serious injuries.

Mark Spitz

Record-Breaking Olympic Swimmer

Young talent

When Mark Spitz was two years old, his family moved to Hawaii and he went swimming every day. In 1956, the family returned to California and at the age of nine, Mark started training seriously. While he was at high school, he held national high school records in every stroke and at every distance, but his greatest strengths were freestyle (front crawl) and butterfly.

Winning at Swimming

In 1966, age 16, Mark won the 100-meter butterfly race in the U.S. national championships. This was the first of a total of 24 national titles that he would win. Between 1968 and 1972, he won five Pan American gold medals and set 33 world records. He was named World Swimmer of the Year in 1969, 1971, and 1972.

Olympic Champion

In 1968, Mark won two gold medals for freestyle at the Mexico Summer Olympics. He was disappointed with this achievement as he was sure he could do better. His great triumph came in 1972 at the Munich Olympics. There, he won four individual events in freestyle and butterfly, and three relay races. His record of seven Olympic golds in one competition was unbeaten until Michael Phelps won eight golds in 2008. After the Olympics, Mark retired from competition and had a brief career as a media celebrity.

Name Mark Andrew Spitz
Nickname Mark the Shark
Born February 10, 1950, in Modesto, California
Personal Life He is married and has two sons.
High Point In 1972, Mark won seven gold medals in the Munich Olympic Games.
Low Point In the 1968 Summer Olympics, Mark predicted he would win six gold medals, but only won two.

Yasuhiro Yamashita

The Greatest Judo Champion of the Twentieth Century

Early Promise

Yasuhiro Yamashita grew up in the town of Yamato, Japan. He began studying judo while he was at grade school and by the time he moved to high school, he had already gained his black belt (a sign of the most senior level of skill). At the age of 19, he became the youngest competitor in history to win the All-Japan Judo Championship title.

Many Victories

In 1979, Yasuhiro won a gold medal at the World Judo Championships. Between the years 1977 and 1985, he won 203 victories and was unbeaten in any competition. His achievements during this time included four World Championship titles.

In his contests, Yasuhiro made excellent use of his heavy build and his left-handed stance and he was equally skilled in standing and ground moves. Many of his victories were due to his hold or choke moves, executed on an opponent lying on the ground.

An Honored Teacher

In 1984, Yasuhiro received the Japanese National Prize of Honor and in the following year, he retired from competitive judo. Since then, he has worked as head coach for the Japanese national judo team.

Yasuhiro Yamashita is seen here at the 2008 Olympics in Beijing. He was involved in helping the Chinese men's judo team to prepare for the competition.

Name Yasuhiro Yamashita

Born June 1, 1957, in Kumamato Prefecture, Kyushu, Japan

Personal Life Yasuhiro is married and has two sons and a daughter.

High Point In April 1985, he won the All-Japan Championships for the ninth time in a row.

Low Point In the finals of the 1980 All-Japan Championships, Yasuhiro's leg was broken by his opponent and the match was declared a draw.

Jayne Torvill & Christopher Dean

World-Famous Ice-Dancing Duo

Starting Out

Jayne Torvill and Christopher Dean both grew up in Nottinghamshire, in the UK. Jayne took up skating at the age of eight and Christopher began when he was ten. As teenagers, they both won junior championships with other partners, but their careers took off in 1975, when they started dancing together. Soon they were winning national competitions as a duo.

Taking Skating Seriously

After they left school, Christopher and Jayne started working at full-time jobs, and it was hard for them to find time to practice. In the 1980 Winter Olympics, they came fifth in the ice-dancing event and decided it was time to give up their jobs and concentrate full-time on their skating.

Olympic Triumph

In the 1984 Winter Olympics, held in Sarajevo in the former Yugoslavia, Torvill and Dean won the gold medal for their dance to the music of Ravel's *Bolero*. Their performance was given the highest set of marks ever awarded to an ice-dance routine.

Later that year, they turned professional and could no longer compete in the Olympics. However, the rules were relaxed in 1994, when they won an Olympic bronze medal. The pair also performed in ice-dancing shows before retiring in 1998.

Name Jayne Torvill
Born October 7, 1957, in Nottingham, UK
Personal Life She is married with a son and a daughter.

Name Christopher Colin Dean
Born July 27, 1958, in Nottingham, UK
Personal Life He has been married twice and has two sons.

Michael Jordan

The Greatest Basketball Player of All Time

A Young Player

Michael Jordan grew up in North Carolina. At school he was outstanding at baseball, football, and basketball, but he finally decided to concentrate on basketball. During his last two seasons at high school, Jordan averaged 20 points per game and was selected for the McDonald's All-American Team. At the age of 18, he won a basketball scholarship to the University of North Carolina.

Star of the Bulls

In 1984, Michael joined the Chicago Bulls, soon becoming their star player both in goal scoring and defense. In 1991, he won his first NBA championship with the Bulls, and he later helped his team to win the championship five more times.

Michael stood out from the rest of the team because of his high jumps and his amazing ability to score goals. He is especially famous for his slam dunks into the net.

Later Career

In 1993, Michael retired from basketball to pursue a career in baseball, but returned in 1995 to play for the Bulls. He retired again in 1999, returning in 2001 to play two seasons for the Washington Wizards. After retiring from basketball for the third time, in 2003, Michael has had a successful business career.

Name Michael Jeffrey Jordan

Nickname Air Jordan

Born February 17, 1963, in Brooklyn, New York

Personal Life He is divorced and has two sons.

High Point In 1990, Michael scored an all-time high of 69 points in a game against the Cleveland Cavaliers.

Low Point In 1993, Michael was devastated when his father was murdered. Later that year, Michael announced his (first) retirement from basketball.

Timeline

1914 World War I begins.

1918 World War I ends.

1927 Babe Ruth becomes the first baseball player to hit 60 home runs in one season.

1930 Donald Bradman scores 974 runs in a single cricket match.

1936 Jesse Owens wins four gold medals for athletics at the Berlin Olympic Games run by Adolf Hitler's Nazi Party.

1939 World War II begins.

1945 World War II ends.

1964 Muhammad Ali becomes World Heavyweight Boxing Champion.

1969 Pelé scores the thousandth goal in his soccer career.

1972 Mark Spitz wins seven gold medals for swimming at the Munich Olympics.

1974 Eddy Merckx achieves the "Triple Crown" in cycling, winning all three major cycle races.

1978 Jack Nicklaus becomes the only player to have won all four major golf championships three times.

1984 Jayne Torvill and Christopher Dean win a gold medal for ice-dancing at the Sarajevo Winter Olympics.

1985 Yasuhiro Yamashita wins the All-Japan Judo Championships for the ninth time in a row.

1988 Steffi Graf wins all four tennis Grand Slam titles.

1990 Michael Jordan scores an all-time high of 69 points in a basketball game for the Chicago Bulls.

1991 Ayrton Senna wins his third Formula One World Championship title.

1994 Ayrton Senna dies in a crash during the San Marino Grand Prix in Italy.

1995 Jonah Lomu scores four tries in a Rugby World Cup semifinals game.

2000 Tanni Grey-Thompson wins four gold medals at the Sydney Paralympics.

Further Reading and Web Sites

Michael Jordan: Legends in Sports
by Matt Christopher
(Little Brown, 2008)

They Did, You Can: How to Achieve Whatever You Want in Life With the Help of Your Sporting Heroes
by Michael Finnigan
(Crown House Publishing, 2008)

Twelve Rounds to Glory: The Story of Muhammad Ali
by Charles R. Smith Jr
(Candlewick, 2010)

Web Sites

Due to the changing nature of Internet links, PowerKids Press has developed an online list of Web sites related to the subject of this book. This site is updated regularly. Please use this link to access this list:
http://www.powerkidslinks.com/tcl/sphero

Glossary

amateur Someone who takes part in a sport for pleasure, and is not paid for playing that sport.

backhand A stroke in tennis that is played with the back of the hand facing outward and the arm across the body.

braces Metal rods strapped onto someone's legs to strengthen them.

celebrities People who are very well-known.

defense Protection from attacks. In a team sport such as football, the defense tries to prevent the opposite team from scoring goals.

diagnose To figure out what disease somebody has.

drive A drive in golf is a shot that is a long, hard hit.

home run In baseball, a batter achieves a home run when he or she runs all the way around the bases of the baseball diamond without stopping.

hurdles Small fences that athletes jump over in a running event.

installed Put in place, ready to be used.

kidney dialysis A medical treatment given to patients with serious kidney problems. The dialysis machine performs the functions of the kidneys and removes waste from the patient's body.

legacy Something that is left by someone to the people who come after him or her.

Nazi Party The party led by Adolf Hitler in Germany in the years leading up to World War II.

outfield wall The wall at the edge of a baseball field.

pacer Someone who helps to keep up the pace of a cyclist in a race.

Paralympics An athletic competition for disabled athletes held in the same year as the Olympics.

paralyzed Lacking in movement, feeling, and power.

pitcher Some who throws (or bowls) a baseball to the batter.

polio An infectious disease that affects the brain and spine and which can make a person paralyzed.

professional Someone who is paid for doing something, such as a sport, that many others do as amateurs.

racism Unfair treatment of others who belong to a different race.

relay race A team race in which members of the team take turns.

run A point scored in cricket, made by a pair of batsmen running a short distance.

slam dunk A goal in basketball, scored by the player jumping into the air and pushing the ball downward through the basket.

sprint A short, very fast race.

stroke A way of hitting the ball in tennis, or a method of moving in swimming.

swing A way of hitting a ball hard that involves swinging the bat through the air.

taunting Teasing.

Test matches Test matches in cricket are matches played between national teams.

track and field Athletic sports that involve running, jumping, or throwing.

Vietnam War A war fought between the South Vietnamese government, supported by U.S. troops and the communist government of North Vietnam.

Index